Thinking
About Ants

For Marian Reiner—B.B.
To Allison—C.S.

The illustrations are painted in gouache on Strathmore bristol board.

Acknowledgment The publisher would like to thank Dr. Howard Topoff, Professor, Hunter College
of the City University of New York, for his assistance in the preparation of this book.

Text copyright © 1997, 1973 by Barbara Brenner
Illustrations copyright © 1997 by Carol Schwartz

For information contact:
MONDO Publishing
One Plaza Road, Greenvale, New York 11548

Printed in Hong Kong by South China Printing Co. (1988) Ltd.

97 98 99 00 01   9 8 7 6 5 4 3 2

Designed by Sylvia Frezzolini Severance
Production by Our House

Library of Congress Cataloging-in-Publication Data
Brenner, Barbara.
    Thinking about ants / by Barbara Brenner; illustrated by Carol Schwartz.
        p.   cm.
    Summary: Asks the reader to imagine what it would be like to be an ant, describing what
ants look like, what they eat, where and how they live, and more.
        ISBN 1-57255-210-7 (hardcover : alk. paper). — ISBN 1-57255-209-3 (paperback : alk.
paper)
        1. Ants—Juvenile literature. [1. Ants.] I. Schwartz, Carol, 1954- ill. II. Title.
QL568.F7B655   1996
595.79'6—dc20   95-45990
                                                                          CIP
                                                                          AC

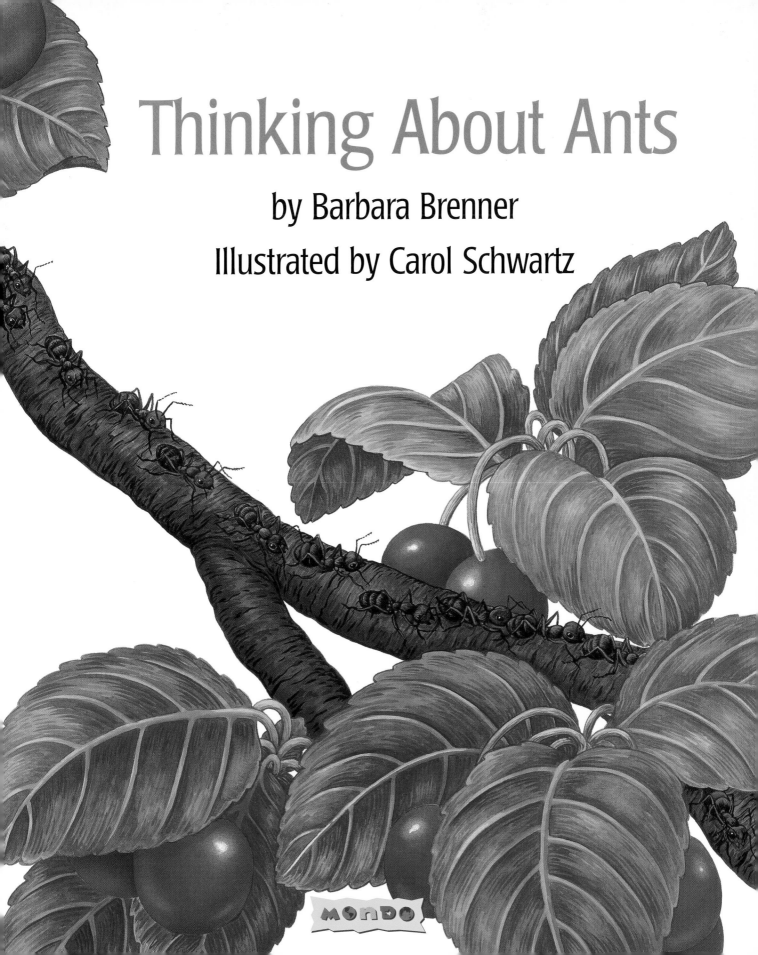

Thinking About Ants

by Barbara Brenner

Illustrated by Carol Schwartz

MONDO

Now, here's an idea.
For a little while,
think about ants.

Begin by looking.
Get up close to an ant.
Study it.
Try to put yourself in the ant's place.
Think, *How would it be, to be an ant?*

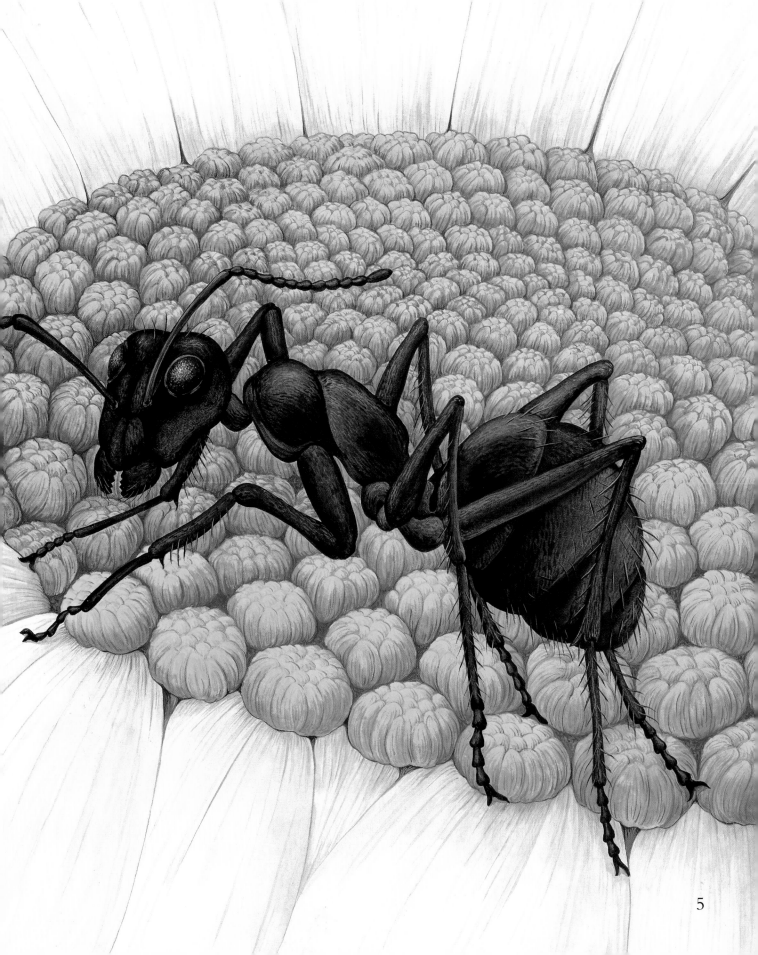

First of all, think small, because
the largest ant in the world
is only about the size
of a person's thumb.
And some ants are small enough
to hide inside an apple seed.
So think tiny.

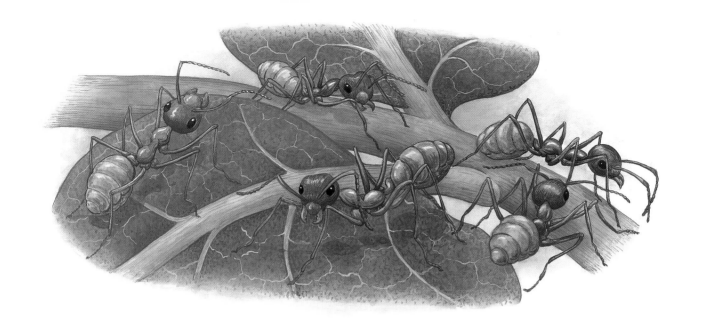

Now think a color.

Black. Blue. Brown. Red.

Yellowish or greenish.

An ant could be any of these colors.

What color ant would you want to be?

Next, think about the body of an ant.
Imagine its outside—light and tough
and hard, like a shell. Not soft, like skin.
Notice the ant's shape.
A body with three parts,
six legs instead of two.

How would it be to have an ant face?
Two huge eyes, a mouth,
a pair of scissor jaws
to bite and tear with.
No ears. No nose. Instead,
two hairy feelers on your head
to wave around like magic wands.
They'd catch the smell
of something in the air, like . . .

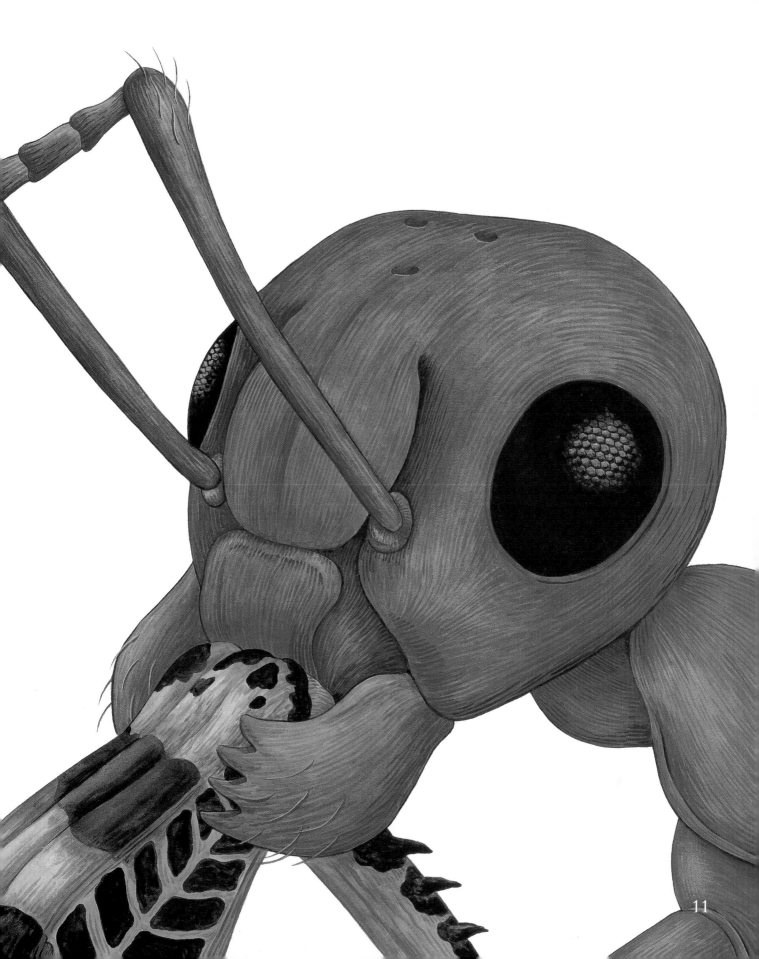

Food!
What do ants eat?
Some eat meat.
A snack of dead bug.
A hunk of worm.
A bite of lizard.
Or an ant will munch
on a piece of hot dog
left from someone's picnic lunch.

12

13

Some ants eat seeds.
Some eat fruit.
Others sip honeydew
from tiny aphids.
There are even ants
that eat each other.

Some ants bite.
Some ants sting.
Others squirt smelly acid
when they're scared.
If you were an ant,
what would you be afraid of?

A stomping foot.
A hungry flicker.
A spiny anteater.
Heavy rain.
Bug spray.
Toads.
But the scariest thing
in an ant's life might be
another ant that's an enemy.

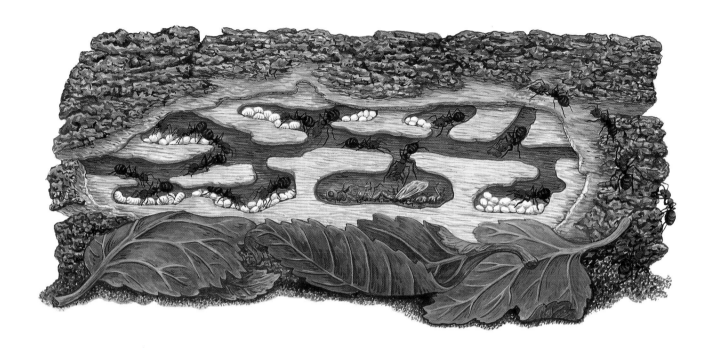

Where do ants live?
In the dark.
Inside a dead tree.
Under a rock.

Under the ground, with a mound
of dirt or sand to mark the spot.

An ant can live in a house
between the cracks in the floor,
or behind the kitchen cupboard door.
Even the green stem of a plant
can be home to an ant.

Think about living in dark places.
But imagine lots of company—
sisters, brothers, a family.
Living and working together because
an ant can't live alone.

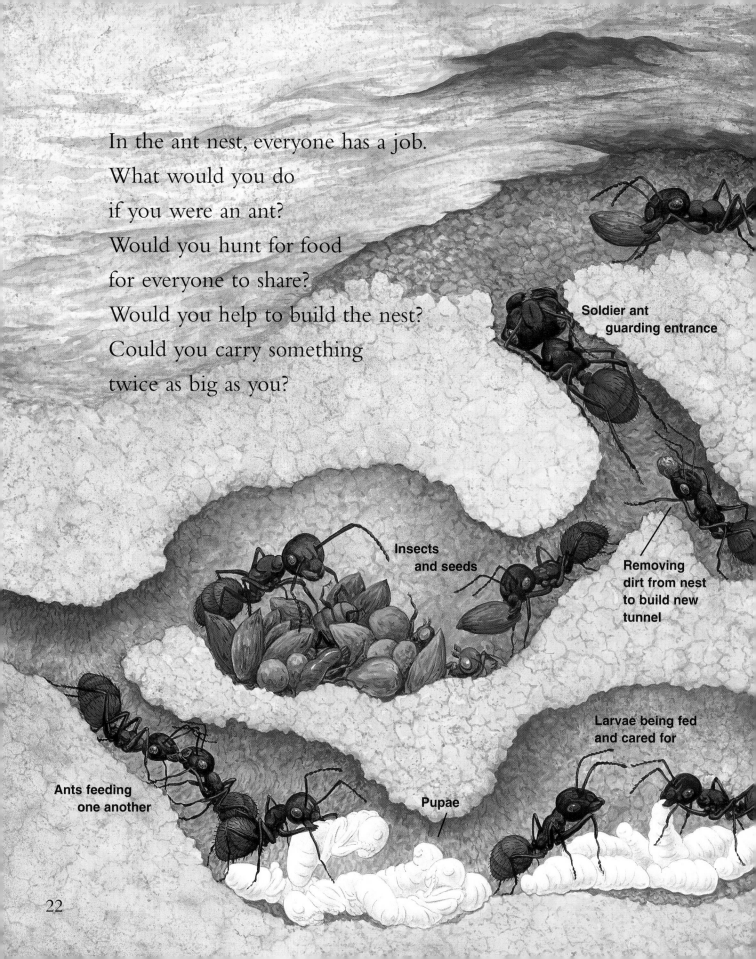

In the ant nest, everyone has a job.
What would you do
if you were an ant?
Would you hunt for food
for everyone to share?
Would you help to build the nest?
Could you carry something
twice as big as you?

**Soldier ant
guarding entrance**

**Insects
and seeds**

**Removing
dirt from nest
to build new
tunnel**

**Larvae being fed
and cared for**

**Ants feeding
one another**

Pupae

Bringing food
to nest

Would you lick the ant eggs
and feed the little larvae
that hatch out?
Would you help an ant
come out from a cocoon?
The ants that do these things
are worker ants.

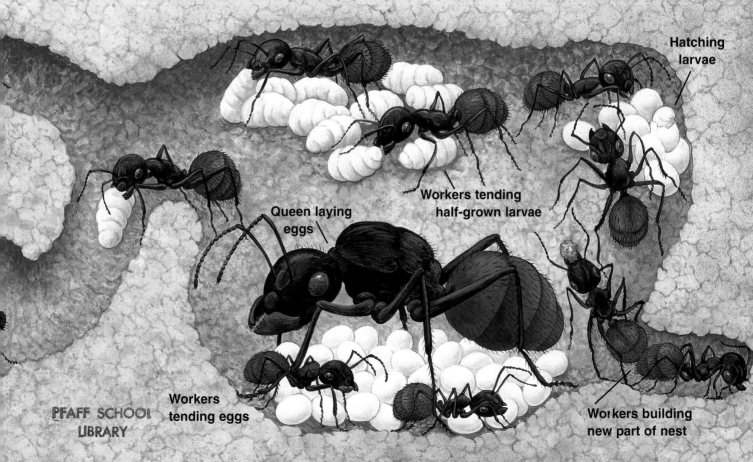

Hatching
larvae

Workers tending
half-grown larvae

Queen laying
eggs

Workers
tending eggs

Workers building
new part of nest

There are soldier ants, too.
They guard the nest.
They stand at the entrance, alert,
swinging their feelers,
picking up all strange shapes and smells.

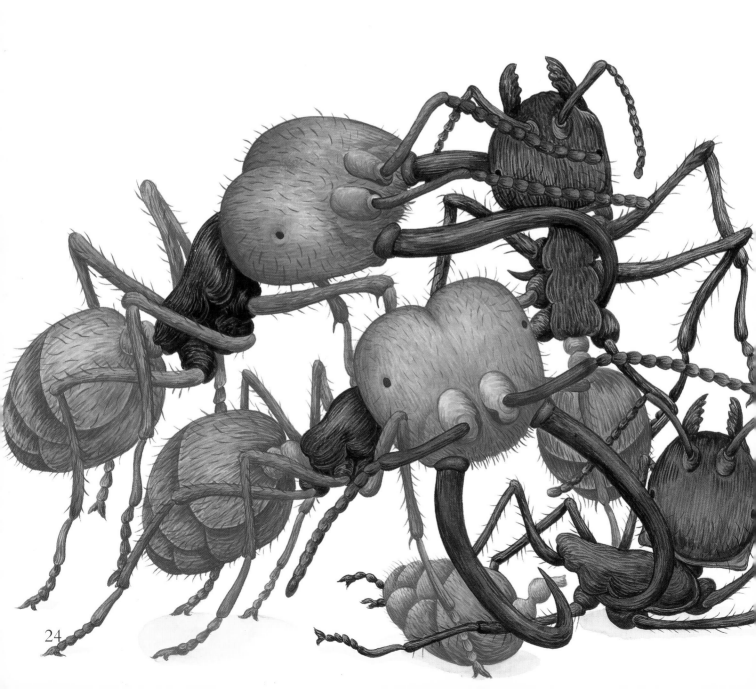

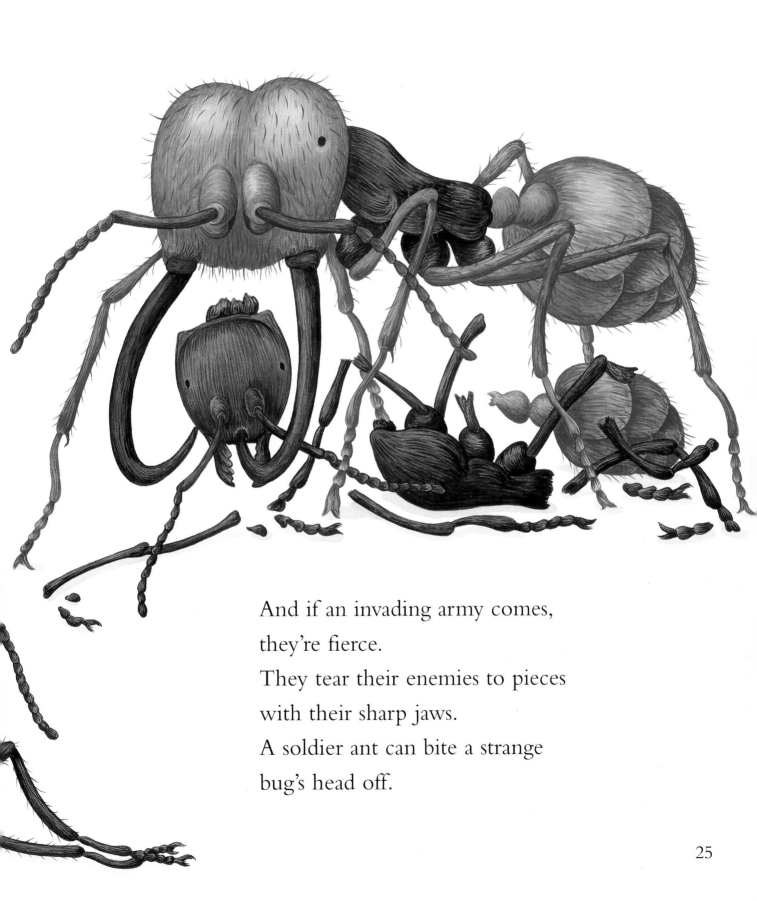

And if an invading army comes,
they're fierce.
They tear their enemies to pieces
with their sharp jaws.
A soldier ant can bite a strange
bug's head off.

Now think about
the biggest ant in the nest.
She's the mother of all the other ants.
She's the only one who can lay eggs.
All the other ants take care of her
because she is the queen.

A queen ant may lay
a hundred thousand eggs
in her lifetime.
One day she may lay an egg
that will hatch into . . .

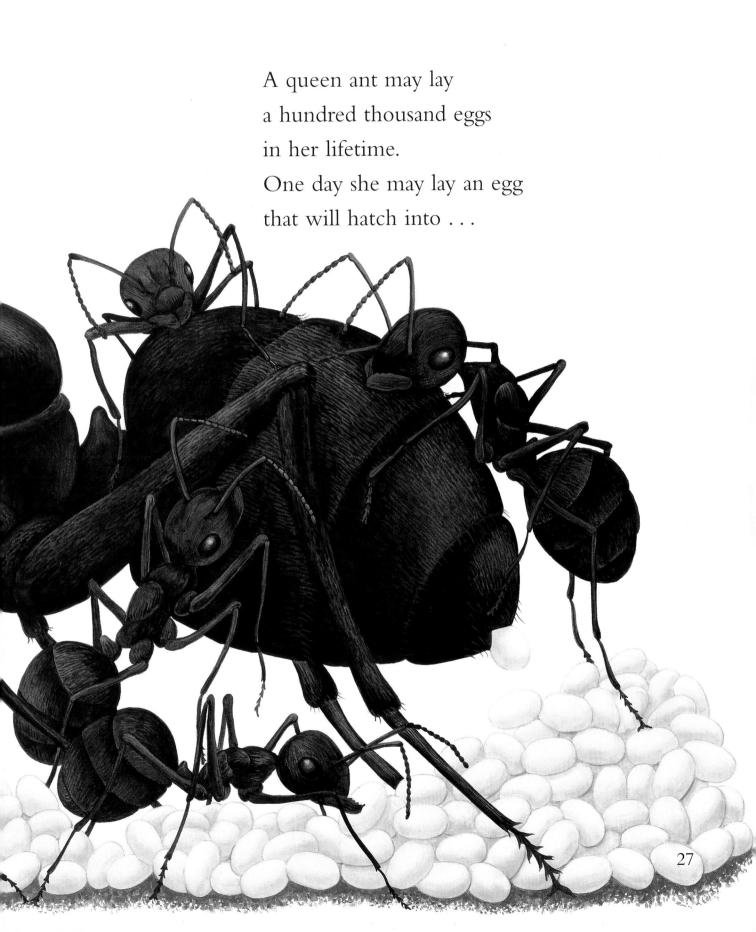

another queen.

Like all queens, that ant will have wings.

Some damp afternoon she'll fly away
with a group of male ants.
They'll mate with her, and
soon after that they'll die.
Then the queen will fly off alone
to make a nest of her own.
She'll lose her wings and begin her work—

Nest-maker.
Egg-layer.
Ant mother.
And some day
she will lay an egg
that hatches out a queen.
Then the whole cycle
will begin again.

That's how it would be
to be an ant.

Ants Shown in the Book

FRONT COVER: Weaver ants carrying honeydew secreted by caterpillar
PAGE 1: Leafcutter ant; worker on leaf
PAGES 2-3: Black carpenter ants on cherry tree
PAGES 4-5: Black ant on daisy
PAGES 6-7: Blank ants on apple
PAGE 8 top: Weaver ants
      bottom left: Honeypot ant
      bottom right: Harvester ant
PAGE 9: on leaf: Leafcutter ant
      on bark: Trapjaw ant
PAGES 10-11: Carpenter ant with grasshopper leg
PAGES 12-13: Black ants with, from left to right,
      lizard, beetle, lacewing, worm
PAGE 14 top: Black ants eating gooseberry
      bottom: Red harvester ants taking seeds from dead flower
PAGE 15: Black formica ants milking aphids
PAGES 16-17: Black ants battling Fire ants; green toad on branch
PAGE 18 top: Carpenter ants in nest
      bottom: Honeypot ants in nest
PAGE 19: Leafcutter ants in nest
PAGE 20: Black ants
PAGE 21: Colobopsis (co-lo-BOP-sis) ants living inside white ash twig
PAGES 22-23: Harvester ants in nest
PAGES 24-25: Army ants from two different colonies at battle
PAGES 26-27: Carpenter ant queen laying eggs; worker ants tending her
PAGE 28: New carpenter ant queen emerging from cocoon
PAGE 29: New Carpenter ant queen with males
PAGES 30-31: Carpenter ant queen digging new nest
      among strawberry plants
PAGE 32: Black ants carrying cookie crumbs to nest
BACK COVER: Carpenter ant queen and workers